My Dog Has Had Puppies

by Leonie Bennett

Editorial consultant: Mitch Cronick

Copyright © **ticktock Entertainment Ltd 2006**
First published in Great Britain in 2006 by **ticktock Media Ltd.,**
Unit 2, Orchard Business Centre, North Farm Road, Tunbridge Wells, Kent TN2 3XF

We would like to thank: Shirley Bickler and Suzanne Baker

ISBN 1 86007 978 4 pbk
Printed in China

Picture credits
t=top, b=bottom, c=centre, l-left, r=right, OFC= outside front cover
Colin Seddon photographer (Kaspurgold puppies): 12-13, 20. Corbis: 4.
Kaspurgold Golden Retrievers (Phil and Susan Hocking): 2, 5, 10, 14, 15, 16, 17,
18, 19, 21. Shoonahs Golden Retrievers (Marilyn Barford): 1, 8, 9, 11.
Superstock: 6-7.

**With thanks to all the dogs and puppies featured in
this book – and their owners!**

CONTENTS

My dog Pip

This is my dog Pip, with me and my mum.

Pip is three years old.

Pip is a golden retriever.

Fat tummy

Pip has got a fat tummy.

Going to the vet

The vet checks that Pip is well.

He looks in Pip's eyes and ears.

He feels Pip's tummy.

Pip is going to have puppies.

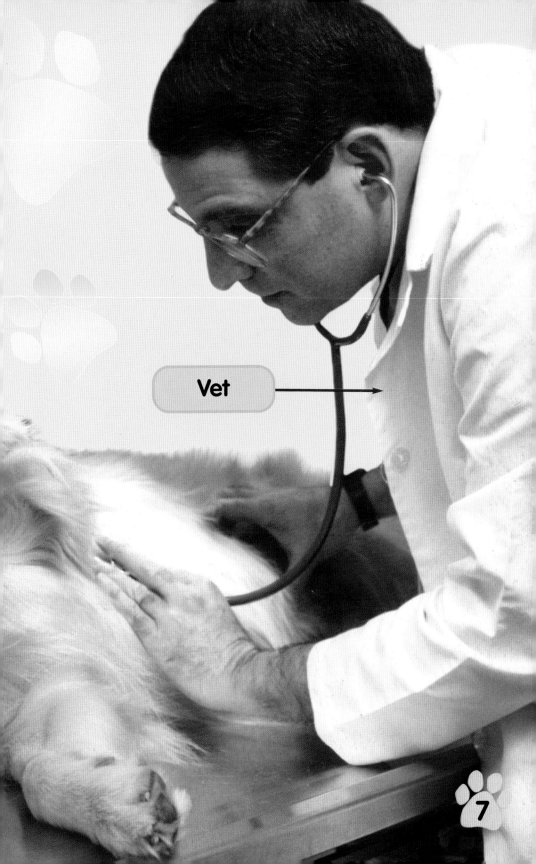

Vet

Wow – my dog's a mummy!

We make a bed for Pip and her puppies.

We put it in a quiet place.

Pip's bed

Blanket

The puppies are born.

One, two, three, four, five, six...

Ten puppies!

There are ten puppies in the litter.

The puppies drink milk from Pip.

Pip licks them clean.

Then they go to sleep.

Look at the new puppies

The puppies are two days old.

They can't see.

They can't walk.

They sleep a lot.

The puppies sleep together to keep warm.

Watching the puppies grow

Now the puppies are four weeks old.

They can see.

They can walk.

The puppies sleep in a big box.

The puppies want to get
out of the box.

Time for dinner

Now the puppies are eight weeks old.

They can eat solid food.

The puppies still like to drink milk from Pip.

This puppy is the biggest.

He eats a lot.

Playful puppies

The puppies like to play.

They like to chew.

The puppies make puddles on the floor.

Sometimes they go to sleep in funny places.

Saying goodbye

Now the puppies are ten weeks old.

This puppy is going
to a new home.

The puppy's new owner gives him a cuddle.

The puppy will ride in this basket.

21

Yes or no?
Talking about puppies

There are four puppies
in the litter.

Yes or no?

The vet looks in
Pip's ears.

Yes or no?

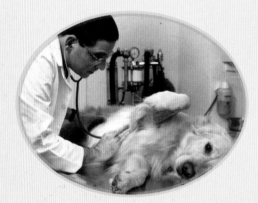

Puppies can
see when they
are born.

Yes or no?

Puppies can walk when
they are born.

Yes or no?

How would you look after
a puppy?

Activities

What did you think of this book?

 Brilliant **Good** **OK**

Which page did you like best? Why?

• • • • • • • • • • • • • •

Put these words in the right order:

going • puppies. • Pip • is • have • to

• • • • • • • • • • • • • •

Make a big poster to show that there are some puppies for sale.

• • • • • • • • • • • • • •

Who is the author of this book?
Have you read *My Cat Has Had Kittens* by the same author?